Background Check

How to Do Your Own Professional Background Search

by Valerie McGilvrey

© 2014 by Valerie McGilvrey All Rights Reserved

No portion of this book may be reproduced or transmitted in any form whatsoever, including electronic, mechanical, or any information storage or retrieval system, except as may be expressly permitted in the 1976 Copyright Act or in writing from the authors. Requests for permission should be addressed to:

Investigative Resources
P.O. Box 1906
Montgomery, Texas 77356-1906

Connect with Valerie on LinkedIn
Valerie@McGilvrey.com
Twitter: @skipease

Check out Valerie's blog at TheDailySkip.com where she blogs about current investigations and skip trace tools.

Legal Disclaimer:

This volume is not legal advice. You must know your federal, state, county and city laws regarding the legality of accessing credit and background checks for your specific purpose. For instance, California prohibits accessing an applicant's credit report for a background check for the purpose of employment. Names have been changed, but the stories are real.

Version 2.1 Background Check
Published May 21, 2014

ISBN-13: 978-1481237611
ISBN-10: 1481237616

Need a background check... but need it today?

I can help you with that.

I can provide elements of the background search with same day service.

Credit Reports
Criminal Record Searches
Arrest and Conviction Searches
Asset Searches
Locate Current Place of Employment
Verify References

I also provide credit reporting services for the purpose of collections. If you're the creditor of past due accounts leverage your collectables with reporting that to credit.

Please contact me personally.
VALERIE@PENRR.COM

To all of the very careful and concerning parents and employers.

Table of Contents

Introduction...11

Background Check 101...16

Landlording...25

Social Security Verification...32

Driving Records...36

Vehicle Registration...39

Credit Records...42

Criminal Records...48

Education Records...55

Court Records...58

Worker's Compensation...61

Bankruptcy...64

Social Media...67

Personal References...77

Medical Records...92

Property Ownership...81

Military Records...85

State Licensing...88

Past Employers...95

Sex Offenders...100

The Interview Method...103

Forms...108

Links...126

Credits & Colophon...137

Introduction

There are over 1.9 million people in United States prisons for drug and alcohol-related crimes. People with criminal convictions have rights. However, business owners and landlords have the right to investigate and owe a duty to the neighboring residents to not have a convicted felon living in their community. Business owners have liability and insurance requirements to satisfy and because of this duty, we do background checks.

What happens to your company if you hire someone without a background check and over $25,000.00 disappears collectively from your client's holding accounts? It happened to I.T. Management Services. Before the owners revealed to employees that missing money was known to them, every employee in the company was investigated.

Any person who had access to any accounting, receivables and disbursements received a background check. I was assigned a background check for an employee of the company whom we'll call Sally.

Sally was a perfect, punctual employee who managed condominium properties for I.T. Management Services. Her job was to collect monthly maintenance fees from the condominium owners and pay vendors such as lawn care, garbage services and the pool cleaner.

As I processed every detail in the background search, I saw that she bought a brand new 2003 Mercedes Benz just six months prior to the discovery of the missing money. Sally also had a theft conviction in 1999 in another county, a county she had not lived in since her conviction. The timing of the new car purchase was in perfect alignment with the company's accounting discrepancy. This wasn't a detail that was shared with me until long after her conviction.

When I brought the findings of my background check to the owner, he seemed shocked. Sally drove an old beater Ford Taurus to work every day. From there, the CPA audited every account that Sally had access to and discovered that large checks were being written to a landscaping company which was registered to her brother, and her name was also on the account. Checks for unauthorized work and most likely for work that had never been done.

Sally had been paying fake invoices as a vehicle to embezzle money directly from condominium communities and spending the money freely. Records showed that Sally put a $10,000 cash down payment on the car of her dreams and when the car was seized it had less than 2,000 miles on it. As it turns out, Sally never made a payment on the car after she bought it, and she was scared to death to be seen driving it.

Sally was nailed. She went to jail, and the car went back to the lien holder. The management company's error and omissions insurance repaid the stolen money, and restitution was court ordered to be paid by Sally as a condition of probation. The real moral of the story is you cannot judge a book by its cover. Sally appeared to be a hardworking church lady who always was quick to offer prayer and comfort to those around her in need.

What tipped off the company to the whole scheme Sally put into motion? A repo truck was seen driving the parking lot and talking to the security officer. The repossession agency specifically asked for Sally by name and offered the security officer a nice cash reward to call him if the Mercedes Benz ever up showed up.

The office manager's main concern for an employee having money troubles would be that temptation and likelihood of taking take a bribe or stealing money.

Background Check 101

Who can do background checks? Most companies that do background checks are not detectives or private investigative firms, but actually deep research firms that specialize in doing background searches after obtaining a signed authorization from an applicant.

Unless the county or state in which you plan on hanging your background search shingle says otherwise, you don't need to be licensed in any way to perform this business-to-business service.

Alternatively, doing the checks for your personal reasons and your company doesn't require any special licensing either-only permissible purpose and skill. If you are doing your own background check and you uncover information that is negative and does not come from a reliable source, I do recommend that you hire an outside investigator to confirm your findings. You don't want to deny someone on the basis of some information you uncovered then come to find out it's not actually them and you're getting sued.

The signed release should detail what type of information is being accessed and researched. You may not care about a person's credit score but if you have the waiver signed and in the employee file you have future background searches legally covered.

A questionnaire on an employment application or tenant application should ask specific questions about criminal convictions, driving records, educational degrees, and so on. The verification process would be at least expected to cover those areas of history inquired about on the application.

Background checks can also be done after the hire. If you are planning to give an employee more responsibility over valuable merchandise, control and access to sensitive and confidential information or access to large sums of money, then yes, you can do a background check at any time in the duration of employment.

The signed authorization forms that the applicant provided when first hired are continuing authorization to do a background check at any time without notice to the employee.

If you see a red flag that makes you wonder about an employee, put your fears to rest. You, as a property owner or employer, deserve peace of mind and need to be able to trust the people around your children, living in your investment home and representing your company.

Looking for criminal felony and misdemeanor charges that have not yet been convicted are as simple as calling your court house in the county which your business is or your subject lives. I see many of these open cases becoming available online within city or county websites.

Who needs a background check? Any person that you don't have firsthand knowledge of their character. Any person that you would entrust with money, children, elders, property and any other aspect of a business or property where you can suffer an loss and also is covered by insurance.

Hiring someone without doing a background check is an act of negligence. An applicant's history must be documented to protect the employer from negligent hiring. If the person you hire commits a crime in the scope of employment, without a background check, the company is legally liable.

You must clear someone who works caring for children and elders, works any type of job that takes your employees into a customer's home or client's property.

There are far too many children as crime victims in the news today. Stories detail sexually and physically-abused children at day care (or in someone else's care) by someone who has a history of being child predator. Why wasn't a background check done to screen out criminals?

A person who is given the responsibility of handling money of any amount or living in a community where the neighbors fit the profile of the tenant's past crime victims is a concern. The extensive background check can range widely from identification verification to learning a person's entire history.

For a company, whose new employees receive expensive and specialized training; the routine of "here today and gone tomorrow" can be not only frustrating, but time-consuming. Background checks give a human resource and hiring manager the peace of mind knowing that you have done everything in your power to research this person. Ensuring the fit is right for your team and the person has the moral ethic you want to represent your company, babysitting your children or living in your rent house.

Would it be illegal to ask an applicant if they have been convicted of a criminal offense? In some places it is. The counterbalance of not asking about previous convictions would be having a signed release with specific language authorizing the potential landlord or employer to look for arrest records and criminal convictions on a nationwide level.

A deeper search for all the places that an applicant has once lived would be needed in order to uncover hidden convictions or arrest records.

Use a database that would provide every address ever associated with the social security number and date of birth. A professional database such as Findmyskip.com, Accurint.com or Masterfiles.com can provide a long and accurate history of what addresses and counties the applicant has previously lived and give you other cities, counties and states to conduct the background search.

Because databases gather information from many unusual sources and update at different times you should have several of them. Magazine subscriptions, credit header information, insurance applications, pizza delivery customers, mail order mailing lists and change of address are just a few of the places databases receive information.

The best and most affordable professional databases are listed in the Links chapter of this book. Some even have very accurate criminal records searches that are very up to date.

An alternate move would be for you to require the applicant to bring to you a certified criminal history search from the county in which they live along with a fingerprint card done at the sheriff's office. This is an authorized government document and puts the applicant's fingerprints on file and possibly in a computer system so the identity of the person can be discovered if fingerprints are matched from a crime scene.

 If you have a true criminal on your hands, you will know it when the applicant is a no-show for the next meeting or deadline for gathering those documents.

As an employer, you may be lenient with someone who has had a drug conviction, but as a landlord, a history with drugs is out of the question, and the opposite could be true for theft. As an employer, you would not be able to hire someone who has a theft conviction but as a landlord this is an acceptable conviction to go forward with your contact for leasing property.

Should you, if you discover an undisclosed criminal record, disclose this new-found information to the applicant? What if it wasn't the applicant's criminal record, but a person with a similar name and date of birth? If the question were put to me, I would examine this on a case-by-case basis.

If the employer feels the employee is qualified for the position, and this is the only thing standing in the way of hiring, then yes, you should go the extra mile to verify that this is indeed the applicant's criminal history and not someone else's. Go to the courthouse, look at the mug shot or have an investigator do this for you. If you like the applicant then at this point you may consider discussing the conviction in detail. Ask questions and don't be shy.

The situation out on the table could give you the peace of mind that you need to continue with the hire. Only in a meeting where you want to hear the applicant look you in the eyes and talk about the past will give you the answers to the all important question: Will he do it again?

What about retaliation? If an applicant believes that the job was not granted to him on the basis of further investigation into undisclosed information revealed in a background check, you could be the target of retaliation. Better to be safe than sorry. You are not under any obligation to disclose findings. The rule would be to verify and confirm with an outside source that the reports are true and correct.

Keep your disclosures to the applicant generic. Just simply stating that the budget for a new employee has changed or someone else was hired without your knowledge by another manager could be some good parting excuses followed by many, "I'm so sorry!" apologies.

Landlording

The most important aspect of pre-qualification of an application for leasing out your property is determining if the prospective tenant can afford the rent. Documentation for this would include check stubs and child support pay history, and benefit award letters from the government.

Word of caution: don't calculate any income your applicant claims, unless there is proof. When $300.00 a month is paid in child support, request documentation that this money is paid to the applicant by requesting a pay history from the Attorney General's office from where child support is disbursed. You should be able to see an online printout or check stubs sent by the disbursement office.

Ask for bank records for a minimum of the past three months. Reviewing a bank statement with copies of checks and check card purchases lets you know where your applicant shops and gives you a bigger picture of money management. Have they been paying rent to someone else?

How are they going to get your rent paid? You also may have a personal preference for someone that doesn't make daily trips to a liquor store.

When your applicant signs the authorization form and receives the disclosures, it will be known to him that a background check will be done. Most landlords pass this expense along to the applicant as an "application fee".

Tenant screening includes all the regular screening actions plus a few extra steps of contacting personal references and family members that the applicant puts down on the reference sheet. I suggest getting about ten references. Five of those should be family members and the other five friends of the applicant. Make sure that you get entire names, full addresses and telephone numbers.

When you check your applicant's references, you will be calling and confirming the address on the reference sheet as well as asking for a secondary contact phone number. I do this because the phone number that the applicant gives is usually a cell phone number that is not in service when I need to make contact with a reference to find my tenant has turned into my debtor.

Rejecting applicants is an embarrassing and sensitive area for some. No one likes a confrontation. However, if you discover information that will exclude an applicant from being a qualified renter other than poor credit history, finding the words to explain can be a hard thing. My only concern would be any discrimination against age, race, religious or political affiliation.

Keeping the rejection to a professional standard of communication is recommended. Sending out a letter that states, "We are unable to rent an apartment to you based on your credit report from Experian", and then give Experian's address so that they may see what is on their credit report. Lack of rental history as well as poor rental history is a standard reason for rejection.

Alternatively, you could say that you are deeply sorry, but your husband signed a lease with a family without your knowledge. This statement (could be a blatant lie but also is a good excuse) gives you damage control, keeping the rejection unemotional and down to the fault of your "better half". In my case, I would just want to make sure I don't tick someone off and become the target of vandalism or arson.

Kinsmanship with other landlords is normal. I always call a landlord listed as a rental reference knowing the conversation may be one-sided and all for the applicant, but sometimes underlying information that turns into an important topic will slip out in natural conversation.

If your rental reference wants to talk shop, let him. I think that when you sit and listen to what someone has to say you're rewarded with pay dirt at the end.

Sample questions:

- Keep up with the yard and landscaping?
- How many times was the renter late with rent payments?
- More than 30 days late with rent, more than 60, 90?
- Property damage?
- Leave the property clean?
- Lie about pets?

In disclosures, I suggest having the applicant initial the statement explaining that renter's insurance is not provided by the landlord, and the personal property and contents are the responsibility of the applicant.

All appliances are noted in the lease with serial numbers and photographs. This is for theft prevention. Contractual agreements mostly are viewed in court as if something is not included then it's excluded.

So, if you don't name that washer and dryer as your property and as a part of the lease and they disappear you might not be able to do anything about it when they go missing in a middle of the night rush move. Especially if you don't have proof that you bought them.

Failing to report water leaks is a reason for early lease termination with tenant responsible for balance of the lease. As well as many other clauses that are outlined in your lease contract.

In case of emergency notify contacts also help you in the event you have to get someone served in person and the tenant is evading. I know that many courts will allow a constable to post on a front door but when a relative is served on behalf of the renter whom you know has contact with the tenant, you're more likely to get some action on part of the tenant.

Independent landlords must be self-reliant. If you reach the point where you must file an eviction go ahead get a judgment at the same time. Another landlord may know to check the county records for judgments and past evictions and then will find your case. I recommend contacting a collection agency that reports to at least two of the three major credit bureaus.

There are smaller agencies that will do a contract for collection with you with no upfront fees so the debt will be reported to credit, and you have a better chance of getting paid because a renter will have to pay you to get into another rental property.

Social Security Verification

The old trick of swapping around the last four digits of a social security number to hide past negative credit information has been overcome by all credit reporting bureaus. This trick doesn't really work anymore. If you suspect that the social security number for your applicant is a fake or fictitious number, there are some things that you can do to get all the versions of a social security number the applicant has ever used.

The key to uncovering those variations of the social security number would be to determine if any fraudulent information has been given on the application. The only consideration you should give any variation of a social security number is that of a married person and human error. One method of discovery would be to request a document with the applicant's social security number on it. You can ask for a passport, medical record, benefit award letter or statement of earnings from the Social Security Administration.

When two people who are married or living together apply for credit jointly, sometimes a database will grab one social security number and pair it with the partner's name. This swap is not deliberate and you can determine if that's the case by doing a simple database address-only search without using any names or other identifiers.

This search gets you a list of every person that has ever used that address and if there's a social on the record then most likely the record is from a credit application of some kind and you can see what number was used.

What you are looking for are other names associated with that social security number who lived at the same residence with the applicant at the same time. You may also see when you do the motor vehicle search that there was a vehicle bought together or real property indicating there is no intent to commit fraud.

Using professional databases such as Findmyskip or MasterFiles will allow you to do a social security number only search. With a social search you'll be able to see who is associated with the number and all addresses connected to that social security number.

You might also see older records for the person who the government assigned to that number before it was issued to your applicant.

These databases will allow you to run an address only to see who else has lived there in the history of the address. If a husband and wife living together for many years is the honest answer, you'll find out this way.

Note: When looking into databases to discover places the applicant has lived in adulthood, keep in mind that these professional databases are mostly based on credit information. If the applicant never applied for credit using that address, it may not show up at all.

Another method of discovering where to look for dirt on the applicant is the geological breakdown of a social security number. The social security number assigning method is now completely random to prevent fraud and provide privacy. However, most adults have a social security number that's based on the old method. The link below is to the government's explanation of how the former system worked.

http://www.ssa.gov/history/ssn/geocard.html

Driving Records

When your client schedules the first interview with the applicant, the key documents should be gathered and photocopied. One of those things is a driver's license. Make sure that the client enlarges the driver's license so that all of the small text and numbers are clearly visible on your copy.

Every state has different requirements for obtaining someone's driving history. An insurance underwriter may be directly online with the department of public safety or DMV that handles the driving history record-keeping and access. You may have to hand-deliver the request to a specific office or mail the request. In some states your only option for gathering this information is through a licensed private investigator.

Since I live and work in Texas, I will use Texas as my guideline. Other than looking for indications that the government document is a fake or forgery, on a Texas ID, there are 13 numbers that overlap onto the edge of the driver's license owner's picture. Those 13 digits are required in accessing a driver's history.

Guidelines for driving record checks:

• When a driving record reveals one or no moving violations in the past 12 months, an applicant is cleared and acceptable to drive company vehicles or drive his own personal vehicle in the scope of employment.

• If the applicant is eligible to drive but has two moving violations in the past 24 months, he may be eligible to drive company vehicles or his own in the scope of employment, with the understanding that the driving record will be periodically checked for new violations.

- Applicants will not be hired if their driving record reflects a current suspended or revoked license, three or more moving violations in the past three years, one DUI or DWI in the past three years, a fatal accident, or leaving the scene of an accident. Reckless driving is also a red flag and would not allow the applicant eligible for hire.

Vehicle Registration

Having access to the motor vehicle database in your state is a pretty handy tool for getting information about someone. Just like in Sally's fraud scheme, I was able to verify that she secretly bought a new car with the date of purchase, the address the car was registered to and also the amount that she paid for the car. Other information that can be discovered is additional notification addresses or if the auto past due for registration. Typically just searching the home address will reveal all of the vehicles registered to that address.

If you have a release giving you authorization to contact any lien holders, you might find a vehicle or two on a repossession list. The only reason that would matter is if they have been out for repo for more than six months. That would indicate the applicant is hiding collateral which, in every state, is a felony called Hindering a Secured Creditor. It's not a crime to not be able to pay your bills but a view of that applicant's ethics.

A motor vehicle database can also assist you in determining if a vehicle is abandoned on your property and should be towed away. If there is someone staying with your tenant for an extended period of time without notifying the landlord and lots of traffic can alert the property manager that there may be illegal activities.

Credit Records

Who wants to see a credit report on an applicant? A landlord, any business that hires in the financial industries, banks, a future father-in-law, brokerage firms and businesses that handle valuables, or a current employee whom you want to promote and give more responsibility.

If your applicant is expected to handle money in any capacity, a credit check is a smart way to weed out the undesirable applicants. Looking at a credit report shows employers whether the applicant has a pattern of poor decision-making in his life that might affect his position in your organization.

Having an employee with perfect credit gives instant credibility. It's a sign your applicant can command responsibility and has horse sense. Sure, bad things happen to good people, and things go into collection status and get reported to credit.

A long unemployed period can explain away collection accounts for outstanding credit cards, disconnected utilities and unpaid medical bills. Unexpected things happen. After all, your applicant is human. Credit checks will ascertain general trustworthiness, but many companies are doing it because they need to bond the new employee.

They're looking for evidence of trouble, big outstanding balances, recent bankruptcies, and the like. Some employers believe people with large debts or credit problems could be a risk for bribes and more likely to steal or commit fraud, which small businesses afford, especially in today's down economy.

Bank account history shouldn't appear in a credit history unless the applicant is in overdraft and delinquent on an account. Collection agencies report this debt with the original creditor information. Unpaid checks also will show up on a credit report too.

I don't think an absence of a credit history will be at all problematic, especially if the applicant tells you upfront that you won't find a lot of information because they prefer using cash. If an employer sees a pattern of late payments, large debts, or other financial issues, they may see it as an issue for specific types of positions.

Seeing that your applicant's credit is a wreck is not really a red flag unless it is coupled with jail time for a criminal office or other unscrupulous reasons for the gaps in the employment history pair up with the negative remarks reported to credit. In this case, you would want to pass over this applicant anyway.

Credit header information is compiled from any credit-reporting subscriber who has pulled an inquiry and supplied identifying information to get the report such as address, phone number, work number and social security number. The credit bureaus take this information and store it on the consumer's credit file.

It normally takes about three or four subscribers uploading the same address for that address to appear on a credit header. Another way the information is compiled and made available after the first use of the information is a separate database complied specifically for collections skip tracing.

Equifax has a skip trace database called First Search. If I go and apply for credit with a car dealership, and the salesman takes my application and calls into Equifax to get my credit score, Equifax verifies my identity by the information that I have provided on my application before giving my FICO score in return.

Without having to out-source to get a full credit report, you can get credit headers online via Findmyskip. If you are just concerned about identity verification, this may provide all the info you need. If you need a full credit report and have a release there are referrals in the Links section.

It's not a common thing to call the credit bureaus and let them know I have moved to a new address. I may not want all my bill collectors to find my brand-new phone number. However, they will if they subscribe to First Search. My auto application to buy a new car with my new information that I give will be in a searchable database tomorrow morning for all my bill collectors to see.

Job hunters and renters know that they can examine their credit for any inaccuracies and fraudulent statements on credit. Those items can be disputed, and they will come off the credit completely while the item is being investigated by a credit-reporting agency. So, if you find issue with an applicant's debt, they have not disputed it, yet, or they have, and it was declared that the disputed item was correct.

Sample question:

- There were issues on your credit with some unpaid debts, would you care to explain?

Criminal Records

Motel 6 is preferred by travelers for on the road comfort and affordability, as well recognized by a traveler named Paul Freeman. Paul only had a small bag of clothes and no place to go when he walked into the Motel 6 manager's office in Tyler, Texas and spoke with Ed Davis, the manager on duty.

Paul told Ed he was a maintenance man, and he needed a job and a place to live. He told Ed he could do anything, and he promised not to disappoint the manager. Ed thought the walk-in job seeker was heaven sent, and he gave him access to the maintenance shack and his own room at the motel with minimum wage with the agreement of on-call availability.

Paul never completed an application for employment or provided any type of identification. Ed felt that wasn't needed right at that moment of hire because when Paul started working around the property, he saw things getting fixed. Paul had a knack for responding immediately and working quickly.

Ed trusted Paul's story from the moment they met if for no other reason, than the fact that the small motel needed exactly what Paul was offering.

It didn't take long for Paul to meet the other employees who also lived on the property. They were all drinkers and had a taste for crack, and so did Paul. Late one evening Paul went to the front desk to check out the set up. A front-desk clerk named Julia Rodriguez was working. Paul was trying to figure out how to get into the cash register and get away with the cash without Julia knowing.

He made trip after trip back to the front desk asking Julia for coffee and Julia obliged turning her back to Paul to get all the coffee supplies out of cabinets behind her and fix his coffee. Finally, Paul became frustrated and jumped over the counter and grabbed Julia by the hair making her open the register. Julia reached for the phone, and Paul took the cash drawer and beat her on the head demanding she stay on the floor until he left, or he would kill her.

Paul was arrested in another employee's motel room and charged with aggravated robbery and aggravated assault. He is serving a life sentence in a Texas prison and upon his release, he'll be sent to Alabama to serve the remainder of his sentence for a drug related murder of an older man in Birmingham. The crime that he was fleeing to Texas to avoid arrest gave him another life sentence.

Of course, if the manager had any red flags from Paul he wouldn't have hired him on the spot. At the very least he would have done a criminal background check and he would've discovered Paul had a long conviction record of drug charges that went back into the 1980's. A wants and warrant search would have most likely revealed that he was wanted for murder in another state.

Searching for the states and counties to look for misdemeanor and felony arrests and convictions can sometimes be two separate offices within a county or state. Currently, I don't know of a database that does a reliable nationwide criminal search. This type of search is only reliable by searching each state. Using free and pay databases to list past residences is an easy action that will give you a residential resume of sorts and lead you to a direction where to do criminal record checks.

The pay databases listed in the Links chapter gives many options for pay and subscription professional databases that are not available to the general public. Any database that is available to the general public most likely isn't current and could be full of incorrect information that is not hand verified and otherwise in direct violation of many U.S. laws on federal and state levels.

Other online background check sites (that freely market to the general public online), may not be able to report a reliable history of an applicant, but it may be an excellent place to start, especially if you cannot get access to professional databases that supply the information that you need to do your background check in a timely manner. This process can be done as an outline to start the hand search for information.

An insurance company may not allow an insured business to hire an applicant because of a crime of moral turpitude, which is defined as, "conduct that is considered contrary to community standards of justice, honesty or good morals". The rationalization is that a convicted thief will more than likely steal again.

Most retail chains will not hire anyone who has a misdemeanor or felony conviction for theft. The actual nature and situation of the conviction isn't taken into consideration either. So that means if an applicant was convicted of stealing a paramour's car in a heated argument or something of an explainable sort, it doesn't matter. Theft is theft and there's no rational explanation for irrational behavior other than mental illness.

On some convictions, a deal is made by the prosecutor for deferred adjudication. That means if the probationary sentence is satisfied, then the conviction will be sealed from view to anyone searching in the future. However, if the convicted person does not take the correct paperwork to the county or city where the arrest occurred, the arrest will still be found in a search. Most people don't know to do this.

I searched the background of a woman who was going to be my son's step-mother and found over 40 criminal cases filed against her for felony hot checks. That kind of worthless check writing is indicative of a street-level drug user.

Her worthless checks were filed by big-name grocery store chains and other stores that allow cash over the purchase. What I didn't find was any conviction for felony check writing, which she should have been charged with, and I should have been able to find. However, to no avail.

When I let my family law attorney know about the arrest record, it came back to me that she received probation with deferred adjudication and she had been released from probation satisfying her conditions. Her record of arrest and conviction were supposed to be suppressed.

If she, who shall remain nameless, had taken her paperwork to the arresting authority, I would have never known she was a serial hot check writer, and most likely a street level drug abuser. Further digging allowed me to find her husband at the time she wrote the checks, who also had felony drug convictions in the time frame of the two being legally married and living together. The only thing it would have saved would have been her reputation, because now I know the truth.

Education Records

This is a very straightforward search. The school's administration office will confirm dates of enrollment and degrees. This includes high school deplomas. If you're confirming a GED you may have a small hurdle as that information can only come from the education agency of the state unless the location of the GED was a college or high school.

All you have to do is call. I have in the past, called administration and registration offices and was given the last date of attendance included with class information. There are a few websites that give you a confirmation of a degree, and I listed those in the Links chapter.

Over the years, I have spoken to investigators about the forged degree claim on a resume or application, and the human-resource department has only been able to catch them because other degreed professionals working in the same office recognize the applicant's claimed college doesn't offer the degree the applicant says they received. When I researched the percentage of reported phony degrees on resumes, it came out to a whopping 45%.

A suggested resource is to look into online Alumni webs sites and to ask for a reference of someone that went to school with the applicant. Social sites such as Reunion.com have merged with the online information giant MyLife.com giving the researcher more history into education than any other online source.

Court Records

Court records are there forever. All filings from the original petition to the final judgment are kept in computer databases as well as detailed in the case file in the court records department. These records let you know who has sued your applicant, filed an eviction and what the outcome was.

It's all public information with the exception of family court matters which you may have to go in person to view. If there's past due child support this would appear on your applicant's credit report. Just like any other past due account there will be a notation of the last time child support was paid and the amount of arrears.

Destructive tenant's judgments may not show up on credit records for a while, if at all. What if you are really renting to someone who was freshly evicted? If you are interviewing potential renters as an independent landlord, then it pays to give your local court house at least a phone call.

My rental property is my primary investment and the cost of repairing the nightmare an unscreened bad tenant left behind is usually more than I received from them in rent total.

The flip side to ending a relationship with a destructive renter is to go ahead and file with your local court and get your eviction on record. If for some crazy reason your tenant breaks back into your property and sets up camp, you won't be able to get them out of your house until the eviction is filed and served.

Without an eviction, under the lease, your bad tenant has legal rights to occupy the property. If you've filed it then you'll have it along with all of the protection that the law gives a landlord in an eviction.

The blacklisting process begins at the level of filing for eviction. This is where other landlords look to find your eviction and judgment for damages. If the renter wants a clean bill with you, he will take care of his obligation so there will no longer be a judgment filed.

Have you ever looked at the Fictitious Names records online or on the court house computers? This is another telling court record search. An important angle is looking to see what business names have been registered by your applicant.

Requiring an employee to sign a no-compete contract that would be an agreement that the employee can't go into business for himself and take your clients away without suffering some consequences.

Looking for business names registered in your county, and the county where he lives along with any contiguous county would be necessary and a good idea if you want to do a check periodically after employment begins to ensure no breach of contract is taking place.

Workers Compensation

If you are not checking for worker's compensation claims, you should be. Employers who don't look for this very important history of claims could cost their company money and possibly make you the victim of a scam artist leaving a history of claims as proof.

Hiring an employee who has had a past injury can also affect the ability to do that job, have a new job-related injury, or put other employees in danger of on-the-job related incidents. State records typically have date of injury, time lost, and employer during the time of incident, type of injury, body part and job related disability.

Suggesting that the prospecting employer have the applicant submit to a psychical exam after knowledge of a prior claim would give some peace of mind. Explaining that the applicant should be checked out to ensure his ability to perform the demands of the job.

It's not legal to disqualify the applicant because you find past claims do exist, but if the injury of the prior claim would prevent an applicant from performing duties of the job or re-injury could cause a new claim under your employment.

Most state's worker's compensation records are public but not available in an online retrieval system. The information you can receive will vary state by state but in general, if you're not able to call a worker's compensation office (usually governed by a state department of insurance or insurance board), you can have a private investigator to check this out for you.

Workers compensation is covered under the American's with Disabilities Act. This basically means that inquiring about past workers compensation claims is not legal until you have made an official offer for employment. Of course, contingent on a background check being completed satisfactorily. A separate document agreeing to a search into past claims would be given to the applicant when you are ready to dig deeper into credibility, health and disabilities.

Bankruptcy

When people file for bankruptcy they're looking to get debt relief and this is allowed by the federal government. Some people just simply need a chance to catch up and not lose everything they've worked so hard for. I personally think it's alright for a person to file bankruptcy in this age of rolling recessions and uncertain employment futures. I see it as proactive management and hopefully will always have positive results.

After all, if a person stays in their bankruptcy plan that means that they are paying their bills on time. However, a person's behavior in bankruptcy could also let you in on some personal decisions that would affect your way of thinking.

Taking in stride that any vehicle covered by bankruptcy protection must carry full-coverage insurance, and the entire bankruptcy case can be dismissed by their attorney or trustee (for non-compliance) because of a lapse or insurance cancellation is a considerable fact.

Bankruptcy cannot be used against an applicant for employment eligibility. While other black marks can be used against you, filing for bankruptcy cannot. Employers are prohibited from discriminating against individuals who have filed for bankruptcy under Title 11 of the U.S. Code. Unfortunately, most folks who declare bankruptcy have other black marks on their credit report long before ever filing.

More interesting information comes in the form of a simple phone call to any federal bankruptcy court. Not only is the information a public record, you can receive payment information, dismissal information and confirm dismissal dates and reasons for dismissal right over the phone.

Another big revealing factor of filing bankruptcy; you can ask for and receive employment information reported to the bankruptcy court directly from the court. You may discover a past employer or address that was not listed on your application and take another step to uncovering crucial information on your search.

Social Media

If you make your business public, the public makes you their business. The news is laden with articles reporting trends using social media in background checks that could be crossing the line. You can find out an overwhelming huge amount of information about someone on their Facebook page.

The ethical rule is that if the social media page is public, then you can view it, and if you can view it, you can definitely take it into consideration. The social media king, Facebook, has had so many changes to the way you can find people and view a person's profile that it has become a standard in online background check research.

You can locate a Facebook profile by looking by name, phone number, email or personal references.

Helpful Facebook Facts:

You can reverse a phone number in the search field (xxx) xxx-xxxx in this format. You can also try searching xxx-xxx-xxxx, and if there is a profile that is associated with that phone number, it'll appear in search results.

The address bar contains the Facebook.com email address. If you notice Joe Blow's email address on the search bar is after the / and before the ? in the URL. So the email address is joe.blows@facebook.com and if there was not a "message" button on the profile page you would have to rely on this formula to send email to Joe.

Joe's Facebook page is not public. All that really means is that all the posts that he makes are private for friends only, or friends of friends. At any time Joe could make a post and change the visibility to a public view.

If you could see Joe's friend list you may be tempted to invite one of his friends to connect with you, covertly of course. I call this Backdoor Friending and it could be considered unethical. If you are going to do it, do it in a secretive and private manner.

There are game players (Farmville, etc…) that have hundreds of friends and will accept any random friend request. Then, seeing that you have connections in common, Joe may accept your friend request and you can check out his posts and pictures. I always take note of street numbers on curbs, license plate numbers and other details in the photo. I tend to think that most people that have something to hide will hide it.

But if Joe feels safe taking pictures of his drunken parties with naked girls and lots of guns and pot (making Joe a very undesirable employee, renter or son-in-law), about the only way you can discover it is finding a way to view his Facebook page. You are looking for problematic behavior that would lead to legal hassles for an employer or a lawsuit for a landlord (not to mention the cost of your daughter's divorce).

What you are looking for:

- Aggressive or violent acts

- Unlawful activity

- Racism and discriminatory behavior

- Sexually explicit photos and remarks

- Illegal drug use

Once you've become connected you might be able to see information in the "About" link located directly under the user profile picture that was not visible before. Other phone numbers, places of employment, and email address found here can be used as search tools (searching in Bing, Yahoo or Google) that will lead you to more information about your applicant.

A word of caution: you cannot use the information you discover on the internet or any social website to discriminate by age, race, religion, disability, pregnancy, medical conditions or political affiliation.

Users can allow subscribers putting all the public posts on your wall so that you don't have to deliberately go there every day. Remember though that the user can see the identity of their subscribers. So make sure if you do this, you are covert and undercover. This means that a profile with a common name and generic picture. Even my own personal profile said I worked for Sonic, until my mom asked me why I was working a second job.

Facebook has also made some privacy changes taking away the option for a profile to be unsearchable and secret. If there was someone you were looking for and couldn't find them before and they actually have a Facebook page, you'll find them now.

LinkedIn is a professional networking site, and the rules are different. This is an employment-oriented "theme park" for job hunters, head hunters and small business owners networking and marketing. A resume is a standard type profile page, and a user can protect their profile and information or make it public.

More common methods of locating sites and pages associated with your applicant are to run names and phone numbers through search engines. Bing, Google and Yahoo all will provide different results so I usually check all three. Other search engines to add to the list are Infospace.com and Webcrawler.com.

Also, I have found that Facebook pages showing up in a Google search is no longer reliable. You'll have to search Facebook for Facebook users, but notice Bing returns web-based selections (in your Facebook search) when Facebook yields no results.

Blogs, mug shots, obituaries where the applicant is listed as the next-of-kin, and newspaper articles are things that I have uncovered on the internet by just searching a name. Convicted felons who have committed high-profile crimes will turn up either in an online blog or a local newspaper article detailing the crime and victims. Just about every small town newspaper has an archive at the newspaper and now online.

On the side of identity theft, obviously two people can have the same name, but the same parents, date of birth and grave site? An old trend for taking a new identity was getting the birth certificate for a baby who died. People with problems look for ways to get new identities and start over. There are quite a few books and blogs that speak directly to people who want to completely disappear from the life they currently have and get a fresh start.

You may not be able to uncover identity theft right away but using a professional database will show the lack of residential history for a person. For me this would raise a red flag unless they have lived in the same place for many years. With this situation, the tax appraisal district would confirm ownership and possibly a utility company would confirm no transfers in service for the time period questioned.

Twitter is a social media standard with a trend of having as many followers as one can get. Twitter pictures are also geo tagged, meaning you can drag and drop those photos into a decoding software found free online, and get latitude and longitude of where the picture was taken. Another useful way to get the entire history of a Twitter account is to convert it into a PDF.

Log into your Twitter account and enter the following URL into your address bar, substituting the user name for my Twitter username, which is Skipease, in this next line:

http://www.twitter.com/#!/skipease

Scroll down the page (or use page down key) to go down to the very first Twitter entry. It may take you a while to get there if you are investigating an older account.

I use Firefox and on the right upper corner of my Firefox browser is a dropdown box with the name Firefox on it. When you click on this box you will see several options, and the one you want to click on is Save As. I save files like this to my desktop so that I don't have a hard time finding it to print or attach to an email.

Lastly, open the full version of Adobe Acrobat. Go to File , create PDF from file. Then select the HTML file that you downloaded (it should be called something like " Skipease (skipease) on Twitter.html and create the PDF. Twitter does have instructions for downloading the entire history of a users account on the site. If you're confused about the process you can get clarification in the help section.

Personal References

Once upon a time, people lived in smaller communities and everyone knew their neighbors. Or so they thought. Living in the same place for many years and creating good close and trusting friendships with neighbors is not totally a thing of the past. With more frequent natural disasters and waves of recessions, whole families are uprooted from their long-time homes and moved into different living situations.

A normal routine for the middle class, one house, two-car family has drastically changed. Resorting to being underemployed, apartment dwellers that need to live close to public transportation to survive or moving in with other family.

Personal references are different from work references. A personal reference is someone that the applicant knows away from work on a personal level. A neighbor, schoolmate, lifelong friend or church family. And of course, those personal references can be co-workers from the past. Speaking to personal references helps paint a picture of what the applicant does and who they associate with.

The ethics of speaking to a personal reference is as important as the reason why a background check is necessary in the first place. What references have to say is far more important than what an applicant says about himself. The purpose is to uncover the truth and reveal undesirable behavior and criminal patters and avoid the worst-case scenario.

Professional work-related references may be chatty about the applicant because they don't have deep bonds with him like a family member or personal friend would. Professional references are people who can comment on the candidate's past job performance. Your questions can get more personal with a professional reference and you can get the dirt you were looking for.

A negative (or even lukewarm) personal interview with a reference can result in an end to an applicant's consideration. A Red Flag response would be along the lines of, "I wasn't asked if I could be put down as a reference." And you'll hear this line ever so often. I've learned if I am patient and listen I'll be rewarded with details that matter.

Drama has a way of working to the surface and you'll be able to detect sabotage right away regardless if it's from a personal or professional reference. Simply ask the applicant for more references.

A list of good questions to ask a reference:

- How long have you known this person?

- How do you know this person?

- Are you related?

- What can you tell me about this person?

- What can you tell me that I might need to know to employ this person?

- Would you loan this person money?

Property Ownership

In a situation of taking on a business partner, looking at property ownership and assessment value is standard in a background check. If owning property is an indication of good standing, then check out the tax appraisal records. Not every mortgage has an escrow for taxes and the property owner has to pay them on his own. Not every piece of property has a recorded lien on it either. Paid in full or owner financed properties included.

Appraisal districts in every county keep tax records that reveal the date the property was bought, taxable value, the school district taxing authority and dates the taxes were paid.

Credit reports can reveal mortgages with a payment history and other loans while listing the type of credit account. You'll see the word auto, home or home improvement loan in one specific place in the record.

The best place to get a guide to decoding a credit report is from the source you receive the report from. I've found them all to be different and a little confusing at first but with some research and experience I learned what goes where and the meanings.

Verifying assets is a factor in assessing future risk. An insurance underwriting investigation would take the same steps of verifying assets to prove up the need for any sum of insurance coverage. If you have a person who is applying for a one hundred thousand dollar insurance policy, the value of real property (regardless if it's secured by a lien) should prove to be the same value.

The basic idea for insuring the life of a future partner is that corporate-owned coverage is needed in the event of a disaster or business partner's death would be to cover the loss of psychical assets or what that person would exclusively contribute to the company as an owner-operator.

In this situation you may request a financial statement to be given to you that would be prepared by a bank along with bank statements and other records of financial investments.

UCC filings are not something that is thought of to search. Now a fully online public record search done on **http://publicrecords.searchsystems.net**

From the site:

"When a secured party makes a loan to a debtor, statement is filed with the state U.C.C. Uniform Commercial Code division. A UCC-1 financing statement notifies others of outstanding debt such as security agreement, summary judgment lien, commercial or maritime lien. Collateral items may be listed on the statement."

Tax assessments and liens are another phase of a financial search done at the county property record clerk's office.

Military Records

In 1970's a man robbed four banks via the drive-thru window on a bicycle. Yes, the teller actually sent him all her cash through the drive-thru tube. He wore the same old greasy, beige work hat with a Firestone logo in every robbery.

He kept up the routine, cycling up to the window just as the bank teller sent out the drive-thru tube and turned the lane's open sign on to start the day's business. The robber sent a tiny little rolled-up note that demanded all the money be quietly sent out to him or the bank would blow up in the name of the Palestinian Liberation Organization. Yes sir, that's right. The PLO.

It took a stake-out with four cooperating police departments to catch him riding away from a Houston, Texas bank drive-thru with the tube zipped up inside his jacket. The reason that no one could catch him was because he was riding around the corner and throwing his bike into the back of a parked van waiting with the motor running and the backdoors wide open.

No one thought to look at any Firestone store to see if an employee fit the description of the bicycle bandit. Stanley Edwards fit the average description of any white male employee working in the entire city of Houston.

It's not likely that he would have been found out and if Firestone had checked Edwards military records, they would have discovered that he had been dishonorably discharged from the Army in that same year. Would it have kept him from being hired? Possibly not at all since he didn't work in a position that handled cash.

The types of discharge statuses are honorable, general, other than honorable, bad conduct or dishonorable depending on what the situation is regarding discharge circumstances. A discharge form, titled form DD-214, can be provided to you by the applicant and the status is noted in block 24 on the form.

If you are looking to find out if someone has ever been in the military at all, call the recruiting station and have a recruiter run the social security number in the database. No-hit means no military involvement. You will have to call the Army recruiting office for Army, Marines for the Marines, etc. It is also illegal to claim military honors that were never given.

I have also had success calling a recruiting station asking for someone to look up dates of enlistment and verification if a person is still enlisted. I've received the base address and commanding officer information along with phone numbers needed to contact the commanding officer.

State Licensing

Certain types of jobs require a state exam and a license to perform. Selling insurance, hair dresser, security officer just to name a few. Laws are ever changing to protect consumers from fraud and create a level of minimum requirements for vocations such as plumbers, electricians and tow truck drivers.

Not having the license doesn't mean that someone can't do the job. It just means that there's credibility in the license process and the license holder has passed a state exam with minimum requirements of knowledge and could possibly maintain a minimum of continuing education classroom hours to keep that license and then there could also be a bond requirement or minimum insurance policy required.

A person may be knowledgeable and capable of wiring a house, but have not taken the state exam to get the license, kept up with the continuing education requirements or pay the license fee to stay current with the state.

If a license expires it's possible that the state would require a new exam and application process be started for that person. The reason it could matter is that there would be more than one license number assigned with a record of issuance and expiration dates.

Interesting occupations that require a license and special type of insurance bond in most states:

- Auctioneer
- Barber
- Cosmetologist
- Air Conditioning
- Credit Repair
- Tow Truck Operators
- Repossession Agency
- Collection Agency
- Salvage Yard
- Storage Lot
- Mechanic's Shop
- Temporary Employment Agency
- Polygraph Examiners
- Court Interpreters
- Water Well Installers
- Pest Control Company and technicians
- Alarm and Video Security Systems
- Security Officers
- Private Investigators

Truly this list can go on and on. I've noticed that on many state licensing online sites that there's an option to search a name through the entire database of license holders both past and present. Just double check to see if a second site that covers different occupations exists and look for county and city level license and permit databases as well.

Medical Records

Medical records of any kind are unavailable to a potential employer, unless there is a signed release for obtaining those records from a specific doctor or testing facility. If the applicant tested positive for drugs in a previous drug test, you will never know.

The only conclusion is to have your own drug test and to maintain sporadic and unannounced drug tests for every employee. Unless you're in a small town and there's only a couple of drug testing labs around and you send the release over to every facility, of course.

All employees must receive the same type of test at varied and unpredictable times. I suggest any drug-testing orders come from an outside office with no personal relationship with the employee. This keeps testing random, professional and unemotional.

Previous medical records can help you evaluate the psychical and mental health of a person for a position where excellent health and mental faculties are most important. With your release you may be able to obtain prescription history from a pharmacy or doctors office giving you a more complete picture of mental health issues.

A specific medial release is required for this type of medical record and it traditionally should be supplied to the doctor directly from the applicant. If you're trying to discover other doctors that this person may have seen then you would need to search pharmacy records for prescriptions and the name of the doctor that prescribed that medication.

State law restricts people from state licensed jobs such as insurance adjusters if there has been a history of mental illness. This is only something that you'll know on a case by case basis but it's helpful to have a general understanding of how to investigate and uncover past mental illness that was professionally treated.

Past Employers

Typically, applicants only reveal past employers that they believe would say positive things about them. If you call an applicant's last job and they tell you that the applicant is not eligible to rehire (a common question put to previous employers), is it all right to push on for more of an explaining?

Of course it is, but it may not be lawful or company policy for the previous job to give you the truth. Their language can influence your idea if your applicant is mediocre or just a bad hire.

Human resource office personnel may have to comply with policies that restrict the questions that can be answered about a past employee. It's possible the only information you can receive will be a hire date and last date of employment.

You could stumble into a company policy situation that doesn't allow a past co-worker or manager to answer job reference questions referring you to the human resources office, and there won't be any one there that worked one on one with your applicant bringing you to a brick wall that not even a signed release will benefit.

If the reason is because the position has been eliminated or another maneuver in restructuring the company, the human resources or former immediate manager may disclose this to you.

However, if it's due to employee theft, lack of punctuality or some other issue regarding interaction with other employees, it may be illegal for them to tell you. I have actually had one general manager plead the Fifth Amendment when asked if they recommended the applicant and if the applicant was eligible for rehire.

For me this speaks volumes and I would place more care and concern into why the information isn't coming forth as a glowing report. In any case, remember to keep a record of who you spoke to and their position, along with the date and time of the phone call with your notes on the conversation.

Another way to discover past jobs is when the credit report is pulled; the last reported job could be listed. Furthermore, people have a tendency to include a work phone number when applying for credit. So if you take all the phone numbers from the credit report and search each phone number (with dashes) in a phone investigation tool or in Google, Bing or Yahoo; a commercial business may be connected to it.

When interviewing the personal references and neighbors, you can ask if they know where the applicant was last employed. Friends are more likely to answer this question accurately, and neighbors may be capable of answering only because they have seen the applicant coming and going in a work uniform.

Getting past an applicant's request to not contact current employer would come in the form of more reference checking. You would never want to hurt a current employment relationship.

As you determine an applicant is or isn't right for your company, making this move when you're directly asked not to could cause them to lose their job putting you in an embarrassing situation.

If you're looking at a person that has a long term employment for a career move obviously a few more interviews and probationary period of employment would be a way to overcome confidence issues.

Truthfully, when a person has a long term employment relationship retired or past co-workers that have a personal bond with the applicant can double as a professional working reference and speak to you in great detail and be able to keep the confidence of the applicant's job hunting activities.

Sex Offenders

I wish I could count on one hand the times I have discovered a sex offender not living at the reported address or in violation by not reporting their new address. It's a felony, and if you check the sex offender registration databases, both free online and with the county or state where you live, you may be surprised at what you discover.

The actual address where a sex offender really lives and stays is only kept a secret when they are still in the criminal element. Again, don't judge a book by its cover. Just because someone looks good and drives a nice car doesn't mean they paid for their own clothes and the car is theirs.

Sex offenders have problems getting rental units in corporate multi-family communities because of the corporation's strict guidelines not allowing felonious offenders to be on property, even as an occupant of an apartment unit regardless of being a party to a lease agreement.

That means a mother can't rent an apartment for her son, a sex offender, and let him live there whether she lives there or not.

Because sex offenders and other convicted felons can't get apartment leases they gravitate toward independent and unsuspecting landlords to have a place to call home. The dangerous side of the situation is that the landlord needs a tenant to keep the mortgage covered on a property and doesn't do the proper background check or credit check to know exactly who is in living in their home.

Some of my former clients have even allowed a renter to move in without getting a copy of a driver's license and other official identifying documents. Not even a completed credit application. Only to discover later the renter was stealing electricity and moved out nearly three months past due with all of the appliances. I've even heard of a renter that took every metal piece of building material out of the house including the garage door.

You need to be able to identify your renters so that if you must file charges on them you can. Not to mention getting your judgment in court.

The Interview Method

The interview method is an extremely invasive way to examine responses to questions that may be highly sensitive to the applicant. It is also a fast way to stop unwise hiring decisions that result in loss and lawsuits. Background check interviews should be done over the phone with a third person not associated with the company. No comments should be made about the company, or client requiring the background check. This would be absolutely unprofessional.

The interviewer should be kind, but not chummy. If the applicant makes comments or jokes about the types of questions being asked, the interviewer should simply restate the question. Methods letting the applicant know the seriousness of the interview should be applied to keep momentum going.

The types of questions you will be asking are in reference to traffic tickets, if the applicant has ever been involved in a lawsuit, either as a plaintiff or the defendant, and other questions where the expected answers would be revealed in database searches, or court and public record searches.

If and when an applicant was arrested and what the disposition of the case was and what criminal issues are currently pending.

While the answers to the questions are important in determining if this person is an upstanding good citizen, the question method is dead-center targeted to detecting lies and the willingness to tell the truth.

If your questions are met with defensive answers stating the question is illegal, or they don't want to answer it, you may need to look into why the applicant is declining. If you're doing this interview in person remember body language matters.

It's understandable that for someone who has been job hunting in today's economy for some significant things in life to go unpaid or passed over. It's more important to put food on the table for the family than it is to pay a traffic ticket. I caution you on the side of humanity to put serious weight only into the truth of the answers.

With this line of questioning you can reveal gaps in employment and other jobs that weren't given on the application.

Sample questions:

- Have you ever hired an attorney?
- Have you ever gotten a speeding ticket?
- Do you have any unpaid tickets?
- Do you owe child support?
- Do you have a warrant for your arrest?
- Have you ever been charged but not convicted of a crime?
- What are all the states in which you have lived?
- Have you ever been hurt on the job?
- Have you filed a claim on workman's compensation?
- Have you ever taken office supplies home without permission?
- Have you ever been in an automobile accident?
- In that accident, did anyone go to the hospital?
- Do you own a car?

- Do you have insurance on that car?

- Have you ever written a hot check?

- Do you have outstanding balances (overdraft) with a bank?

Forms

Investigative and security professionals conducting background, tenant and employment checks that fall under the Fair Credit Reporting Act should check for updated forms and regulations governed by the Consumer Financial Protection Bureau.

The sample forms listed below are suggestions and replications of forms currently in use by other background check companies and landlords. Please consult with your legal department or attorney for approval for the actual documents used in your background check process.

A suggestion for getting completed applications and forms from applicants is making sure that their name is printed where it is signed. This may help a reviewer discover variations of the name as well as covering any legal angles. I highlight the date on all applications because this is something that tends to be passed over by an applicant. If the applicant is accepted as a tenant or for hire, the date on the application is needed for evictions and other processes of legal situations with the applicant.

The PDF format of these forms can be found for a download on learnskiptracing.com

Click on Background Check and then look for the word DOWNLOAD FORMS on the bottom of the book listing. If these forms are not available for a download please send email to **backgroundcheck@cellbust.com** and they will be emailed to you.

CONSENT TO BACKGROUND AND REFERENCE CHECK

In consideration of solicitation of my application for employment, or application for lease of premises, I, [print name] _____ , do hereby give my consent to [potential employer or landlord] _____ , and the authorized agents thereof, to check the references listed on my application, and to check my background in any way, including but not limited to contacting any and all persons and business entities in order to inquire regarding any and all information relating to myself, provided that said inquiries be limited solely to the purpose of consideration of myself for possible employment or tenancy.

Applicant print name: _____

Applicant Signature: _____ Date: _____

CONFIDENTIAL

Print Name: _____

(First) (Middle) (Last)

Former Name(s) and Dates Used:

_____

Current Address Since: _____

(Mo/Yr) (Street) (City) (Zip/State)

List all previous address for the past ten years.

Previous Address From:

_____

(Mo/Yr) (Street) (City) (Zip/State)

Previous Address From:

_____

(Mo/Yr) (Street) (City) (Zip/State)

Social Security Number:

_____

Date of Birth: ____/ ____/ _____

Telephone Number: (____) ____-_____

Drivers License Number/State: _____

The information contained in this application is correct to the best of my knowledge. I hereby authorize (Organization Name) and its designated agents and representatives to conduct a comprehensive review of my background causing a consumer report and/or an investigative consumer report to be generated for employment and/or volunteer purposes.

I understand that the scope of the consumer report/ investigative consumer report may include, but is not limited to the following areas: verification of social security number; current and previous residences; employment history, education background, character references; drug testing, civil and criminal history records from any criminal justice agency in any or all federal, state, county jurisdictions; driving records, birth records, and any other public records.

I further authorize any individual, company, firm, corporation, or public agency (including the Social Security Administration and law enforcement agencies) to divulge any and all information, verbal or written, pertaining to me, to (Organization Name) or its agents.

I further authorize the complete release of any records or data pertaining to me which the individual, company, firm, corporation, or public agency may have, to include information or data received from other sources.

I hereby release (Organization Name), the Social Security Administration, and its agents, officials, representative, or assigned agencies, including officers, employees, or related personnel both individually and collectively, from any and all liability for damages of whatever kind, which may, at any time, result to me, my heirs, family, or associates because of compliance with this authorization and request to release.

Signature: _____ Date: _____

Print Name: _____

Witness: _____

Witness Print Name: _____ Date: _____

Driving Record Disclosure and Authorization Forms

EXISTING EMPLOYEES

[Company Name] will check the motor vehicle records for all current employees on an annual basis. Any employee without a valid driver's license will not be allowed to operate a company vehicle or drive on [Company Name] business. If driving is an essential job function, and the employee cannot be reasonably accommodated, the employee will be terminated. If an existing employee has a valid driver's license, however if the employee's driving record meets or exceeds Probationary Status criteria, the employee will be placed on Probationary Status and will be subjected to the requirements of that status until the end of the probation. If during a subsequent periodic motor vehicle record check, the employee's record indicates further violations, the [Company Name] will review the specific circumstances surrounding the individual and determine appropriate action.

APPLICANTS

[Company Name] will check the motor vehicle records of any job applicant where driving is an essential job function and where a rental car must be obtained for business travel purposes. The applicant's job offer is contingent upon this driving record check. The driving record check will include review

of any appropriate state records based on the employee's application and resume. If the applicant does not have a valid driver's license, the applicant will not be hired. If an applicant has a driving record that meets or exceeds the criteria listed under the Unacceptable Status, the applicant will not be hired. If the applicant meets the Probationary Status criteria he/she will be placed into that status.

Signature _____

Printed name _____

Date _____

[Company Name]

For the purpose of the background search.

The (name of background search company) will assist you in procurement of this job opportunity by providing to [Company Name] verification of your background, job skills, work history, experience and dependability.

CONSENT FORM

I consent to and request that (name of background search company) make inquiries necessary to verify the information I have provided on my resume, application, and during interviews by and for [Company Name]. I understand and agree that (name of background search company) may now, or at any time in the future if I obtain this job, make inquiries concerning my past employment history (to include pay, attendance, dates of employment, and reasons for leaving), medical history, education, financial responsibility, worker's compensation claims history, involvement in prior litigation, and criminal history.

I further request that the results of these inquiries be communicated to [Company Name] and understand that the information will be utilized to evaluate me for possible current or future employment, promotion or reassignment.

Signature: _____ Date: _____

Print Name: _____

RELEASE OF LIABILITY

I understand that the sole purpose of (name of background search company) is to assist me in demonstrating my suitability for and procuring employment at [Company Name].

To accomplish this, I authorize and request that (background search company) contact any or all of the following information sources: former employers, courts, law enforcement agencies, correctional facilities, jails, and all other government record repositories.

I agree that any inaccurate information provided about me shall not be the fault of (background search company) or [Company Name] and that sole responsibility shall be attributed to the source of that information. Accordingly, I hereby release from liability and hold harmless (background search company) and [Company Name] and any contributing firm, individual, government agency, and all of their officers, employees, and agents.

NOTICE: You may write to the (background search company) at (address here) and request the nature and substance of any information obtained from these sources. Please include a stamped and self-address envelope.

Signature: _____ Date: _____

Authorization for former employers to provide information:

I hereby request full disclosure of all information concerning my employment at your company, to include DATES OF EMPLOYMENT, position, pay, and REASON FOR LEAVING. I release and hold harmless all former employers from any damages, claims, causes of action and liability in reference to furnishing and verifying such information.

Signature: _____ Date: _____

Background Check Procedures

(NOTE: These instructions are for management use only; it is not intended for the applicant to see this sheet)

[Company Name] has selected a company known as (background search company) to establish a standardized applicant-screening program throughout our organization. Utilization of (background search company), which specializes in screening applicants for companies all across the country, will make your job much easier -- because it will enable you to quickly identify and hire the best and most qualified applicants.

When considering someone for possible employment, the following steps should be taken:

1. The hiring/department manager reviews the application, interviews the applicant, and determines if the applicant seems to have the necessary skills and work experience for the position.

2. The hiring/department manager explains to the applicant that [Company Name] utilizes (background search company) to verify background information, work history, and job skills that they have provided on the application and in the interview. To give your applicant a reason, if the decision of management is to note hire the applicant, it's very important to be noncommittal and explain that your company is still interviewing applicants.

3. The applicant is instructed to read and sign the "Purpose/Consent/Release Form."

4. Provide to the applicant a telephone, privacy, and instructions to call (background company phone number) for a brief interview concerning their background and job history.

5. The applicant is interviewed (over the telephone) by the (background search company) concerning their background and work experience.

NOTE: The purpose of this procedure will be to determine where the applicant really worked, and the real reasons they left prior jobs. This in-depth background screening procedure delves into issues such as: jobs that were not listed on your application; detailed reasons why the applicant left previous jobs; reasons terminated (fired) by previous employers; if they have ever disputed or appealed the reasons they were terminated (in order to qualify for unemployment benefits); reasons why they have ever utilized attorneys; use of attorneys in disputes with employers; lawsuits and complaints against former employers; criminal history; substance abuse history; vehicular accidents, traffic citations and outstanding warrants for unpaid tickets; history of writing insufficient fund checks and resulting arrest warrants; etc.

6. While on the telephone, the (background search company) instructs the applicant on which laboratory they are to go to for their drug test.

7. A public record criminal history check will be conducted by (background search company) to determine any prior criminal arrest history of theft, fraud, driving while intoxicated, embezzlement, drug/alcohol problems, sexual misconduct, violence, etc.

8. Identifying information shown on the (background search company) report (spelling of the applicant name, date-of-birth, and social security number) should be compared for consistency with the information you have on record. This is to insure that the applicant has not given different and incorrect identifying information in the interview in an attempt to "hide" their criminal history or other negative aspects of their background.

> ➤ If you have any questions please contact the (background search company information).

_____

Printed Name

_____

Signature

Date _____

Links

Please click on these links to print the PDF. Standard procedure would be to provide a copy of the appropriate disclosure to the applicant informing him of his rights.

Summary of Your Rights Under the FCRA – to be given to applicants whose credit you inquire for the purpose of employment.

http://www.ftc.gov/bcp/edu/pubs/consumer/credit/cre35.pdf

Notice to users of consumer reports:

http://www.ftc.gov/os/2004/11/041119factaapph.pdf

Notice to furnishers of information:

http://www.ftc.gov/os/2004/11/041119factaappg.pdf

Pay Databases

http://www.skipsmasher.com

http://www.masterfiles.com

http://www.microbilt.com

http://www.merlindata.com

http://www.accurint.com

http://www.irbsearch.com

http://www.knowx.com

Free (& almost) Databases

http://www.zabasearch.com

http://www.veromi.com

http://www.mylife.com

http://www.pipl.com

http://www.spokeo.com

Useful for Motor Vehicle

http://www.datatraxonline.com

http://www.publicdata.com

Social Security Validation

http://www.ssnvalidator.com

http://www.skiptrax.com

Phone Investigation Tools

http://www.tnid.us

http://www.findmyskip.com

http://www.spydialer.com

http://www.mrnumber.com

http://www.trapcall.com

Credit Reports

http://www.skiptrax.com
(full credit reports and reporting)

Death File

http://www.findmyskip.com

http://www.ancestry.com

http://legacy.com

Sex Offender Database

http://www.familywatchdog.us

http://www.publicdata.com

http://www.nsopw.gov

Criminal Records

http://www.policereports.us/

http://www.publicdata.com

http://www.fbi.gov/about-us/cjis/background-checks/backgroundchk

http://www.skiptrax.com

Education Records

http://http://http://www.degreechk.com

http://http://www.studentclearinghouse.org/

Newspaper Archive

http://www.newspaperarchive.com

Recordsbase.com/obituaries

Other books by Valerie McGilvrey

Revealing tricks, secrets and methods to getting someone found with concise directions from a seasoned skip tracer providing an advantage with big results. Invaluable tactics delve into information and resources not available in any other book. Tools that streamline the process to find the person that you're hunting.

For process servers, recovery agents, collectors and attorneys; experienced and beginners alike. Investigative specialists will appreciate compilation of sites with direct easy-access hyperlinks taking you to the front page of the best skip tracing tools found today.

I have read quite a few investigative books in my career and I grabbed this one on a whim. Quite a few good tricks in here, very detailed and full of ideas that really got my wheels (inside my brain) turning. I know you have to get creative for skip tracing repo's. I think those are the hardest skips out there. They KNOW they are being hunted. Great reference book, and wonderful blog to follow as well. Will be looking for other things by this author.

-Samuel McDurmett, *Houston Scene Magazine*

**The Most Useful Websites:
For entrepreneurs & small business.**
Free CD with the purchase of other books from
LearnSkiptracing.com

This is a brilliant compilation of websites and a book you'll refer to often. Filled with helpful and inspirational little known sites for marketing, sales and business operations. If you're an information hound then this book is the kind of thing that you'll love.

Chelsea White- I've found nearly every website in Valerie's book of interest to me and saved me a lot of time and money. I literally had to click away from every page to check out the sites!

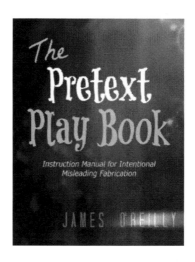

The Pretext Play Book

The Pretext Play Book is a comprehensive guide on the investigative skill of pretexting. Not all skip tracing can be successful with traditional methods, so investigators use hacking and scams to get the information that is the target of their investigation.

Discover pretexts used by law enforcement, skip tracers, repossession and private investigators worldwide. Idea's and Social Engineering scenario's that get results and have hundreds of possibilities. Advanced techniques and modern formulas to trick even the savviest of today's absconders.

Online Orders with secure Paypal Checkout
www.LearnSkiptracing.com

Check or Money Order Payable to:
Asset Management
P.O. Box 1906
Montgomery, Texas 77356

____Background Check….paperback… $10.99
____Background Check…CD…$9.99

____Skip Trace Secrets…paperback…$12.99
____Skip Trace Secrets…CD…$9.99

____Most Useful Websites…CD…$2.99

____The Pretext Playbook…paperback…$16.99
____The Pretext Playbook…CD…$14.99

Payment type: Visa MC AMEX

Card# _____

CVC or QVC (3 digit from reverse) _____

Name on Card _____

Zip Code of Card Address _____

Shipping Address _____

City, State, Zip _____

Credits & Colophon

Valerie McGilvrey
Background Check
This manuscript has been updated to the third edition on May 21, 2014.

Many thanks to all those who helped me with this book, including Bea Blue, for designing the cover page, and my editor Leslie Slaasted.

The screenshots were captured with Microsoft Snipping Tool and optimized for the Kindle with Adobe Photoshop. The book layout was tested on Android, iPad, iPhone, Windows PC, Mac OS X Lion, Amazon Cloud Reader and Kindle 4 (2011 model).

© 2012-2014 Copyright
McGilvrey ePub & Valerie McGilvrey
All Rights Reserved